me

Aunt Jemima

and the nailgun.

me

Aunt Jemima

and the nailgun.

Aziza Barnes

poems

Exploding Pinecone Press
Minneapolis, Minnesota
2013

Copyright © 2013 by Aziza Barnes

This publication is made possible by funding provided in part by Button Poetry and other generous individuals.

Published by Exploding Pinecone Press, Minneapolis, MN, 55408

http://explodingpineconepress.com

All Rights Reserved

Manufactured in the United States of America

ISBN 978-0-9896415-0-0

Cover Design: Doug Paul Case

Cover Photo: Destiney Stubbs

Author Sketch: Rob Gibsun

Where you going?
I don't mind.
I killed my world and I killed my time
…if I live too long, I'm afraid I'll die.

—The Kinks, *Strangers*

I got a head with no screws in it—what can I do?

—Tupac Shakur

So,

me and Aunt Jemima walk into a bar, right?
And she had bit on a mason jar for her nose to fall in,
but her teeth fingers and ears all leapt in the glass,
migrating from their rancid host. By the time
she sat at the bar, ole girl barely had a face.
And my dumb-ass starts giggling right, and I go—
oh no!

I know you.

You bottled shuck-n-jive!

      You Uncle Tom with-a-side-of-pancakes!

You Maid-in-Gone-with-the-Wind!   You Bojangles-
              for-breakfast!

  You Amos-n-Andy-lite!   You self-hate-syrup!

        You slave-gone-corporate!

You black-power-fist-wit-a-hole-in-it!

       You minstrelsy's-mistress!

  You blackface-on-blackface-on-butter!

      You Uncle-Ben's-shawty-on-the-low!

You everybody-mammy!
            You—

Her skin has melded to the bar by now
and I can see thru Auntie J. The muscle
she got left shivers on her bones like a saltfish
trying to understand air. She sits now the one way
I never pictured her:
thin and white. Without eyes, she looks at me hard,

applies a set of lips to her skull, spits—

> quit talking like you know black
> and the box it came in.
> You don't know what it is.
> To smile for all them folks.
> To rot in everybody home 'cept yours.
> To watch they children.
> To hear them call you 'mama.'
> To be hated by your own for trying
> to find a way out. To feed your enemy
> for a century and a quarter.
> To have them profit off you
> while you die slow.
> You don't know me.

I try to console the has-been of Blackness.
Tell her I didn't mean it.
That I'm just a brown girl,
half-breed mutt that don't know her place.
Don't know how to hold her tongue
or respect the dead. I look up at her,
ready to pry out some sweet forgiving,
but my hand is nailed to the bar,
nailed to the chair,
my body pierced in rust,
I cry—
      yo, Jemima, what is this?

Her teeth form a smile at the bottom of her mason jar—

> Rot with me.
> I am your kin.
> You come from me.
> And when they bury you,
> you'll have my face.

Contents

me

Aziza meets Charlie Parker in an unspecified bar on 52nd Street	3
in a jar	4
consider the hand	6
1997	8
hypnophobia	9
brown girl alien	11
my mouth	13
a small act	14

Aunt Jemima

Aziza meets the 4 women: Aunt Sarah, Safronia, Sweet Thang, & Peaches at the Cotton Club afterhours	19
imitation of life	20
the picnic	21
moanin' ode to Charles Mingus	22
a small autobiography	24
at a Mississippi crossroads, Robert Johnson's daughter gets her blues	26
the love unlimited orchestra	27
Juicy (an erasure)	29

the nailgun.

Aziza meets the nailgun	35
lullaby for my unborn daughter	36
Addie Parker Speaks to Charlie Parker, a mother's lost advice	37
a small translation	38
at what/hits stop	39
The Gettysburg Address (an erasure)	40
no country	41
Sing about Me, I'm Dying of Thirst (an erasure)	43
how the world ends/slavery returns to the black man	46

me

Aziza meets Charlie Parker in an unspecified bar on 52nd Street

and she looked at him and he was a forest of floating caskets and that was just in the eyes and she saw his appetites shovel him at the joints and it is frightening to see a wrist mid-excavation the shock the same as seeing your mother naked to see the scars of your birth on her abdomen she can tell he wants to run away but he has at least ten small graves keeping his body at the counter and what she did next was out of pity and there was no behavior to give it a name a name is one of many small borrowings and she wanted to own something that day she took his liter of whiskey broke the bottle into a set of shark teeth and carved a front door into her neck she looked at Charlie and coughed walk inside this city is perishable but it's warm here bird don't you know I would die for you

in a jar

i'm just a set of teeth you know that?
no dabbed lips in compact mirror, no last dance.

i got one piercing on my left ear, it always infected.
cleaning it s'like washing a bullet hole in a window.

you thought this was a stain? ha.
you the same little stupid that thought
water in a jar knew how to be an ocean

once.
maybe twice if it knew how to bite off enuf,
if it knew enuf, knew where the border was.

i don't know a lot of words
once. i demolished a face with a sentence:

well, i'm leaving.
and i think that's what an ocean is,
crash me with what's in me.

i'm a fair fight. one set of teeth on top
of its opponent, they twins, sea on sky. i see it now:

the world's just one big mouth.
that's why we hate the ugly things.
an infected earlobe s'like swallowing a cavity.

we don't have enuf time left
to witness a foul meal. i front porch

with house chewed off. i woman,
muscle screwed down to sweat. i just
try to please the water out.

you know you lose 21 grams the moment you die?
s'like losing 5 teeth.

consider the hand
after Aracelis Girmay

Consider the way a tumor holds:
sweat through, as in a coal miner,
or chilled in back alleys,
outside of a club and myself,
wiping an old night off my face.

If there was a fist here, give it another name:
a coiled Christmas light, blackened. A prayer,
a spider in the pantry; harmless, unrelenting.
The way love isn't.
The way a cancer doesn't know.

It is the one on my lap at funerals,
folded down in a church,
letting some sour God get sick of some sour me.

It is the one that cannot reach my mother
when she cries in the car.

There is a small callus,
unwanted patches of hair,
the stark resemblance to a crab:
all the fixings of a high yella
and a high yella's daughter.

Everything written is 10 years too old.
A coward, it crawls out of a nail bed
and makes a wrong turn, missing
a chance at the mouth.

I blame the right for every packaged silence,
for every brewing "no," hammering in the wrist,
for every blood it dreams to expel
in a strained silhouette victorious,

for holding yours, for calling it "nothin',"
for holding yours, for calling it "home,"

and what a funny happening.
I've made two brothers unmusical somehow.
The left is not the same.
It is some woman's thing used so often
I forget it's there.

1997

When you're 5, your sister
will stare only at objects.
The body associates
with like-matter. For a month,
the non-breathing will resemble
a 20-pound girl with a blue face.

Her doctor is a handless blacksmith.
Whatever he administers
was engineered by faith,
is at the mercy
of what you will cling to.

From that time, you will not
remember any sound: your father's
voice, the axe-picked march of mucus
out of his daughter's chest,
the doctor's shuffling steps, (which
you imagine are small coffins, clapping
the way to your sister's room).
All of these will be hollowed out
for you. The body, for all its holes,
likes to protect.

Your sister's lungs will be returned to her.
Recovery is a forgetful God. The radio
will become an appliance of torture.
For the next year, you will clap off-beat
to every song. The music gnawing
at the fences around your ears.

hypnophobia

Someone is choking you while you sleep.
Your English teacher. The one who
wears those awful khaki pants that show
his manhood everything. He cackles over
your bed, your skin, that hot piece of coal.
Someone must've cut the wire, the one
connecting your brain to your backhand.
Not even an eyelid will save you. He hears
your heart. He can't stand the pulse of it,
the off-putting way you want to save yourself.
He rolls up his sleeve and tunnels his arm
down your throat, uproots your heart,
says to you, "eat it."

You are an unstitched doll learning her parts
as she loses them.

I am not afraid of the night. I am afraid
of its obligation: to close your eyes
and unleash that tight fist of knowing.
I could not have been born this way.
For every fear, there is said to be
a triggering effect. Someone holding a gun
saying, "this may be my fault, but it's still
your story."

A fear of sleep is a fear of losing control.
In my hometown, there was a girl up the street
that knew every part of you is a mouth—
"Look at you! How open you are.
Your body can only say 'yes' to me.
Look how your fight forgot you."

I can never land a punch in my dreams.
Never rip my attacker apart nail by nail and see

how helpless that house was. I'm not a fair fight.
I don't know a lot of words. I don't know
how to say "I slept with every man after you
and woke up on fire." I don't know how to say
"Everyone in my dreams is borne of you."
I don't know how to say "You cannot have me.
Not now. Not again."

"Do not sleep by yourself. There must be
some part of you that don't trust the rest
of you. Find someone who don't
wanna gouge out her eyes to make sense
of the dark." This was never about finding a savior
to share the bed with. I am not lonely.
I am not the weak calling my sickness
the tyranny. What I fear is what I can't hold.
What I would win the world for.

brown girl alien

You have no idea
how bad I want a 16-wheeler
right now. A blue raspberry Slurpee
in left hand and one-o-dem trucker hats
that says "John Deer" or some
such fiction, maybe a pair-a overalls—

that might be too much.
But the sentiment is strong,
like Bourbon-stink. Gosh,
how delicious the Midwest sounds,
like a fat watermelon in August.

I wanna drive past stacks of nothings—
tumbleweed nothings, crab grass nothings,
cactus nothings, sand nothings. Nah,
I don't want the Midwest after all.
I want the I-90 to the Joshua Trees.
Maybe a vulture-picked carcass to stare at.

I wonder, when the aliens dig up all our sacred,
will they be as confused as I am now?
Will their questions be my questions?

What animals were these? The kind
careful enough to preserve the body
of their beloved or the kind selfish enough
to play dress up with their dead?
Or the kind sad enough to say,

"shit, what's this road for if you're under it?"

And I'd drive on miles of I-don't-know-
what-naturally-grows-here-but-if-I-keep-
moving-maybe-I'll-forget-how-I'm-gonna-

lose-you-one-day-no-wait-look-at-the-air-
(a gravity nothing)-look—

look at it go.

my mouth

a cavity of red.
a handful of yes.
a mother, but not quite.
the pit, not the core.
sex, surely. something
I got from my mama.
a mama, absolute. light
as muscle. honey as instrument.
faith's internment. sin as verb.
a womb littered with teeth. collateral
for sound. the inside of lamplight.
a 60-watt bulb, stained. a fistful of belt,
rusting. dirty as a street corner.
dirty as blood. dirty as memory.
something you grow out of. into.
a wound laced with noise. Luther Vandross
on repeat. the sun's attempt at skeleton.
a domesticated violence. a handcuffed ocean.
a root, mid-riot. a root, electric. a root,
viral. a root, distracted. a root, unplugged
and soaked. a closet of lust. socket of breath.
a basin clogged of promise. bolt. the spine's
response to holding. joint gone pulse.
joint gone rogue. joint gone.
something biblical. a verb. hometown
slapped on a body. unedited psalm.
a warm inheritance of bones. tender hook.
line of hooks. slaughterhouse moonlit as church.
grandma dancing with a broom to Footsteps
in the Dark. broom as husband. broom as want.
a strangled trail of notes. desperation incarnate.
buttoned-up vinegar. a zoo of hymnals.
field of callus, beating. a road, condemned.
a road, eulogized.

a small act
for Audrey Hailes

blues bands from Mali, half of a grapefruit,
toast saved from burning, earl grey and honey,
lavender soap, a shower, cocoa butter cuz you bit
your lip, it's okay. it's okay.

hot water, prayer being breath alone, apricot jam,
white t-shirt instead of a towel, wooden
kitchen table, brushing your teeth,
one thing at a time, a bad Richard Pryor movie,
laughter boiling and fine out of the throat,
first laugh in a month, rice and cardamom,
whiskey sours, the sexiest drink to order,
reading Oscar Wao out loud, the first chapter
of something, buds of tea brewing,
cocoa butter cuz you bit your bottom lip,
it's okay. it's okay.

looking at the eye of your own storm,
ordering Indian food instead, Beth Israel,
in a waiting room with a math major from China
who can speak better Spanish than you
even though you look Boricua
and that makes you mad, your phone
taken away, please put it in the bag,
you can get it later, maybe, depending,
"don't worry, I'm here, just outside,"
old woman in wheelchair across from you
dancing in muddy Cantonese, loss
of a translator, green smocks, it's
okay. it's okay.

"don't worry, your sister's here, just outside,"
bodega flowers' quick decomposition,
men with faces so chocolate you gotta make

a song 'bout em and shout it on the 6 train,
pennies, hospital bracelets with your name,
DOB, knowing who you are without instruction,
breathe, okay, try again,

Nostrand Ave, forgetting your government
and becoming brown girl on Macon Street,
wheat beer, Sankofa Aban, shea butter
for your hair, brownstones on brownstones,
looking up at all the visible stars (seven) and saying,
"I guess I'm still here," beer, the good kind,
feeling blood on your busted lip, it's okay.
you're still here.

Lilith's Brood, how one story becomes
another thing, then another, then
too much, then just blood, 9 calls
from your mother, 9 calls from your father,
it's okay, it's okay, I'm still here,

yes, you are, unexpected sunlight,
cocoa butter on your lip, you bit your lip.
you did it on purpose.
you kept on your bracelet.
you will take it off. hot dinner,
half-cut ginger root, Earth Wind & Fire
album covers, your breath, in Brooklyn,
just now, just this, this small act,
this staying here.

Aunt Jemima

Aziza meets the 4 women: Aunt Sarah, Safronia, Sweet Thang, & Peaches at the Cotton Club afterhours

and Peaches was pissed like always cuz Sweet Thang was in the back fucking her man against the main generator making all the lights burn something foolish for the 3rd time that week and Aunt Sarah was this close to cutting off everyone's hands with her bare mouth you forgot music came out of there for one throat there are so many faces it's easy to lose one on a sour note and there was Safronia and I was gas-drenched in a room full of lit matches Safronia you read me to the muscle teach me this our thing your eyes are a manual I don't have I laid my whole finger on her I wanna be seen by the bastard we are Safronia snatched my face and the lights came strong and the end of the world grew an arch in its back gave itself four mouths and a bitter blood spoke this, "what song you got? You five foot meaningless lil mix breed high yella how-you-pronounce-your-name red bone mulatto homeless daddy what do they call you?"

I opened my mouth wide and watched the air fall out

imitation of life

Sarah Jane got legs.
Two well-defined lies
pull her mother's black body
through the snow—dusk
clinging to sugar cane. Under
a street lamp, Blue Eyes catch
her weathered hands on
Sarah Jane's ankles—shackles on
white pillars, crumbling. Her skin
is an unruly organ. Tonight, ink
cannot swallow blood. Blue Eyes,
a lover in strange heat, tangles
Sarah Jane into a brick wall,
beating her until blood curdles
around those legs—his hands,
red and fooled. Sarah Jane
is an ox cursing the weight
of her plow. Her mother's grip
blisters at Sarah Jane's last words—
"If we should pass by on the street,
don't recognize me." At the funeral,
her black body is pulled by four
white horses. Sarah Jane's voice
bucks through the crowd—
"She's my mother!" No response
from the coffin: a dead woman
keeps her word. Mahalia Jackson
sings, sweeps the procession on—
Sarah Jane's legs never matching
the snow.

the picnic

in a Sunday dress in Mississippi I learn the word picnic comes from a funny tradition bring the kids, Johnny! just got his first pair of long pants the checkered blanket freshly ironed, Johnny! pick one! you're old enough! in his formative years, Johnny! supposed the rope grew out of the back of their necks whatever it was it was it was a muscle meant for you to grab with all ten knuckles pull twist tight let it swing, Johnny! didn't get his father's name the second-born everyone called him Sissy! he walked like one the unwanted son-of-a-butcher his family would tutter we were supposed to throw him out, Johnny! you can't catch one in a flock! be patient one will get lost they are good at ending up in the middle of two sweaty palms make sure they're yours, Johnny! grab that one the high yellow in a yellow dress catch fetch go, Johnny! go I feel a burning tug on my wrist a boy wading in his long pants what's your name, Johnny! her hand ain't the holding kind catch, Johnny! he slapped the back of my neck feeling for a growth I thought you were made for this no, Johnny! this is my good dress I only get one a tree is a dirty thing to play on pick one pick one catch, Johnny! be a good-for-something, Johnny!'s family eats a watermelon I watch from the tree til all the red is gone out of me til they are down to the bitter rind I'm sorry for the blood on my dress, Johnny! wasn't it a pretty dress, Johnny

moanin'
ode to Charles Mingus

     sumthin' bout a boy from Watts
     make him talk in third person,

"my boy was a heartbreaker,
taught his women to beg for more!"

     sumthin' bout a girl from Los Angeles
     make her understand boy from Watts
     maybe cuz my girl knows she
     wouldn't put up with his narratives
     'em both native to nowhere,

"my boy—that yella one there!"

     yella is 108th and Century Blvd.
     yella is Crenshaw and Vernon.
     yella is that sweet stink noise grown folks
     slap together when nothin' good on tv.
     my boy knew that sex like the last shred
     of notes shaved fine on a dying bass strung out
     and tight would give it to any broad who asked
     my girl listen to her mama (yella is Clemson
     and La Bera as much as anywhere) tell stories
     bout yella how it make the walk home a parade
     of bricks n bikechains n milk cartons no escapin' it
     smilin' yella make people wanna spill sumthin' loud
     it's a place as much as it's a skin,

"my boy goes back inside himself."

     my girl wonder if he ever made it back out
     my girl got educated in a boy from Watts
     towering over his own face he has all of them
     so he is the most alone my girl wanna know

    where all that high yella walk to
    when it come down when you aint worth
    the last sound crawling on your mouth,

                                  "don't leave, boy…"

"my boy in other words is three they're all real."

    my girl got educated in my boy,
    never got taught to beg for more.
    sumthin' bout my boy break my girl's heart
    make her understand the long walk home.

a small autobiography

Miles Davis had a huge forehead but/was not known/for it

which meant/you would only know to look/at it if you had seen it

of quilt and crowbar/his legacy is

meaning/you must remember/St. Louis and the Midwest

all I see/are cows when I write that

cows and Idaho

by Idaho I mean potatoes

all I know of Idaho/is what grows underneath it

and wasn't he/such a pretty boy

marinate til the fibers tear apart

what funeral were you always/dressing for

I would only know to look/for it if I had seen it

how many times have I seen Miles Davis die

marinate til all the fibers tear apart

I mean I guess/it's just a question of desire

what do you wade in Davis

the dewy-eyed merchant you is

what tore you up/

would I only see/it if I knew to see it

if I had/seen it before

are you trying to tell me something

I am supposed to already know

all I know/of you is what grows underneath

is what marinate til all the fibers

dressed for a funeral you

already know don't you

you playing that horn

you are dressing sound for its funeral

all I know is/I would only know to look/at it if I had seen it

trust me Davis

I've seen men die before

at a Mississippi crossroads, Robert Johnson's daughter gets her blues

Mama taught me there are rules to a man. One: don't ever knock the bottle outta him, and two: if you meet one who smiles easy beware of the teeth. Remember a mouth is a glorified hand and he'll want to root through yours like you ain't got fingerprints. Like you ain't woman enuf to leave a stain behind. You won't see him swig down water. He ain't made of it. She told me all a man got in him is poison, crawling. You smell his kind a delta away, try and keep him that far too. His final hour? S'underneath his tongue. Like a switchblade in a dress shoe. "Don't' dance with a man made of strychnine! All he got for you is music!" My daddy, Robert Johnson, he had music. And when he left, he was more than just the stain a woman leaves. My mama took down her house nail by nail after he left, after his suits got all itchy standing still in her closet like a headline in a sweaty fist. He left with our house. All we got left to live under is his name. Now I'm here, tryna make my own deal cuz I wanna be more than just a unwanted curl in a hairbrush. I wanna knock a bottle into me. Dare anyone to push me. Dare anyone to think my land is just a compliment to his boots. Knock me out and I'll call my hell hounds. I'll have someone to call alright. Someone with teeth.

the love unlimited orchestra

I am the only one who ever lived that remembers Barry White or murder.

I am the only one who ever lived that remembers sex.

I am the only one left.

The last of us is me and all I am good for is remembering.
A dusty record licks a needle with a long tongue.

I lick dust and remember Barry White.
Barry White and murder.
They are not the same but they are all I have left.

A crux of bodies, churning into sound.
Sex is this also, and that is all I can hold in my head.

How impossible an activity.

The small creak and push of a flimsy eyelash on a saucer.
How can Barry White come out of this?

It was before I knew about a touch, voiceless.
The end of love, a chord set to crack.

No fire, no sound.
Only the faint hope of body.

All I was to invent in this life is there in the case files.
My impossible: No dead man can sing.
Lick the dust.

Remember. The impossible: that two bodies
can be so close, they forget,

as long as forgetting allows.

My impossible: Barry White is dead.
No one will have sex again

because Barry White is dead.

Juicy (an erasure)

[Intro:]
    All

        grip.

Yeah.

    All me.

Nothin' lived above.

        Buildings called on me.

    Feed my all

  all

[Verse One:]

All.

 I used
my every attack;

        My red match.

Remember,
you never

    take

now.

'Cause sin,

                I used to.

Call.

      If you don't

[Chorus]

hold,

      I'll give you

[Verse Two:]

change.

        All day.

Keep me.
Miss me.
Play me close like

    life without
    ears.

                I dropped all.

[Verse Three:]

Dead
money handles
one-room.

                        On her back,
            of course.

My face,

no
    heat.

                Why we thirst?

all...

                (all)

don't

you know

the house

mad?

the nailgun.

Aziza meets the nailgun

I don't know how to wait for rain the way other folks seem to. I open my mouth. Foreclose the light. Scream. I can't see past where I got hit. I'm not a lock. Not a needle. Just the afterthought of torque. A good wrist and precision. A domesticated violence. I know what I have: the inside of a stain, a shipyard of want. A hand on your name, then off. I design a wound and it's my best feature. A door, for one. The house blames rust on me. I can't make anything stay put when all I'm good for is making things stay put. Sometimes, I breathe so fast I become a different thing. What I'm trying to say is: you are not the first. I've made my mother cry and couldn't make it stop.

lullaby for my unborn daughter

begin at the blood/when the house is rotting/

at the red summer/when you were too undone to love/

at the high lyric/when you got up out of your skin/

at a low moan/when your mother was a long hand held out/

at that small impossible/when air was loud grease/

at your name/when you did everything to stay/

at the red summer/when you got up out your skin/undone

at the blood/when air was that small impossible/hand

at the high lyric/when you became your mother/loud

at your name/when it was a house/rotting

at that small impossible/love/a skin undone

at the blood/when rotting/became air

at the air/that small house

at your too undone/when a hand held out/was impossible

at the blood/when you begin/to love

Addie Parker speaks to Charlie Parker, a mother's lost advice

Syncopation means
knowing what pocket
to hide your breath
not playing every note
loudly like a man
lost in his own body

a small translation

soy borracho/you're drunk
sí soy borracho/yes you're drunk
borracho pero eres linda linda/drunk but you pretty pretty
entiendes?/you understand?
linda!/pretty!
sabes?/you know?
mírame/look at me
please/please
eres linda sabes?/I don't know
linda!/pretty!
eres linda linda/how to take care of myself
sabes/how to lock up
pero soy borracho/how to shred light simple
se que tu eres linda/how to hold a shrill coil of yes
entiendes?/how to sew without blood
entiendes/I don't understand
eres linda sabes?/no
linda!/I don't have anything left to give you
sabes?/you know?
mírame/see this, all spoiled
soy borracho/you hear?
borracho pero eres/what you want
linda!/tastes better
mírame/silent

at what/hits stop

At 9pm off the Utica stop, you can see a playground gone ghost. A car flooded with soca and an old woman yelling into her Bluetooth at an old man yelling into his Blackberry.

I see her, one foot poised in a Sunday best heel, the other curdled in a slipper sock.

A gold ring decks each finger. I can only focus on extremities. The man is just a man, layered in sweaters and a practiced slouch. They could be talking to each other. They are close enough. They are staring at their feet, the beginning of a strained two-step.

Maybe.

But nah. Not tonight. There is a chill from another winter and I cannot name the soca tune playing, I only know I'm supposed to know it. The way I know a dance that refuses a body is fear sucking dry some muscle. Past Utica is Ralph, then Rockaway, then I walk past the couple that isn't a couple, past a thought about the end of a line, an extremity gone ghost. I hear that soca tune, then watch it drive off into Lewis Ave and I turn right, shake off possibility, stop trying to remember the title, where I heard it first, when I was close enough.

But not tonight.

Down Lewis, a man hollers at me, "aye yo! yo ma! I'm so attracted to you— can I please take you to the steak house?" The man is just a man and I know I'm supposed to know it. That we will not talk to each other, but yell at possibility. That we'll get mad at what we have to grow out of, at what hits stop.

The Gettysburg Address (an erasure)

This all

                Might live.

But we?

                        Cannot

    Cannot

                Can

      not.

no country

1.

Is there a word for:

Just-a-brown-thing
no-sound-no-home
mother-loud-name
call-it-a-family-call
me-a-joke-daddy-can't
open-him-mouth-without
a-lie-searching-for—

Just one?

2.

Grip my hand on a phantom home,
all I do is ride out.
Hand it over!
The Vegas you know
is bitched to dust
and all your women squeal
in my fist. Call me some other name.
A Chief, a Soldier, a Brown Mockery
of Your Dead God.

My demands are few.

3.

Engineer a neon hate for me.
Crash it quick and call a SWAT Team
from 1976. I want to be so bad

they name a gun after me.
Rattlesnake and Tired Whore,
a dangerous respect I will dole out
for they have known my skin
and that is the lowest me.
Stuff every black baby in a djembe.
Watch them beat a way out.
I decree this racket a clock tower
and every cell phone's ring tone
in my province, for it is more than me.
Birds of paradise from my ma's wedding
bouquet will flock my desert. My kin.

Dear fools,
you don't know me.

4.

Slice your eyes shut.

Yours truly,
Officer of the Armageddon,
Black Columbus of the First World,

chokes the curve out of her horse's back,
her tears unmaking Nevada proper.

Sing about Me, I'm Dying of Thirst (an erasure)

(Sing about me)

[Intro]

[Verse 1]
I'm
        not
           here
I can

borrow   my mind

I find nothing

      is what

we consider
      A bullet

will whisper,

"like you

           I knew thunder"

whenever

I tell

        the lights

    about

[Verse 2]

You.

A swallow

       of my

          damaged system.

These homes

            used to be
  one room
in vain.

I am enough

     of a waste.
Fade
the grind.

     Sell this light

        down. Shut off a

[Verse 3]

mirror. Today,

        rake the wound.

    Tongue your

           real like

[Hook]
promise.

[Skit]

(Dying of Thirst)

I was once
a rupture
of water.

how the world will end/slavery returns to the black man

there is a gas station that is responsible

for you/the year is 2051/we made it/

thank you for that/Mayans regularly sacrifice

again/they came back/wear Boy Scout uniforms/

and carry pitchforks/made up in powder/they worship

the image of Michael Jackson/because more copies

of his face were found than that of/Jesus/

they all assume/he was our most worshipped

God/I don't have the heart/to correct them/

I pump gas at this station/that is responsible for you/

they put me in electric blue heels/made out

of the Caribbean coastline/what's left of it/

is in the fabric/gripping my left ankle/don't know

where they drained the rest/although women do

look a lot more/water/logged these days/

their eyes/are not responsible/for you/

in that way/they are unlike this gas station/

no woman here knows/of your blood/the brimming

of it in your/shot-out lids/like a drive-by/

this/you are responsible for/actually/

the only way/I am able/to speak to you/

the only way/this conversation is possible/this

is happening/because I am/pumping/

you/into a car/they operate/on your antibodies/

every car is/responsible for you/you

drive the masses/

Notes

Notes on the erasures:

"Sing About Me, I'm Dying of Thirst " is track ten on the album *good kid, m.A.A.d city* (2012) by Kendrick Lamar.

"Juicy" is a single off of the album *Ready to Die* (1994) by Notorious B.I.G.

"The Gettysburg Address" is a speech given by Abraham Lincoln in 1863.

I want to give thanks/blessings/praise to the following folks whose hands touched this manuscript and helped to make it exist: to Sean Mega DeVignes, Safia Elhillo, Camonghne Felix, Ishmael Ish Islam, Mahogany L Browne, Beau Sia, Michelle Denise Jackson, Alexa Velasquez, Alex Key, Yarminiah Rosa, Josh Smith, Jon Sands, Angel Nafis, Shira Erlichman, Donny Jackson, Murktarat Yusuff, Audrey Hailes, Connor Sampson, Taylor Simone, Rico Fdk, Libby Olga Howard, Rachel Zucker, NYU's Undergraduate Creative Writing Department at Lilian Vernon on West 10th, Slam NYU, Sybil Cooksey, Mike Mlekoday, Samuel J. Cook, Dylan Garity, Michael Lee, and the entire staff & creative team that is Button Poetry/Exploding Pinecone Press, Button Poetry for existing, being fly/generous/brave and allowing me time/space/freedom to build this work, to Bao Phi for reading this joint. For saying "yes." And to Machelle Bailey, Craig Barnes, Sarita Barnes, Stephanie Barnes, Gary Stephenson and Sebastian Rivera, aka, The Family, the Original Ride or Die.

About the Author

© Rob Gibsun

Aziza Barnes is a brown woman poet from Los Angeles currently living in New York. She is a senior at Tisch School of the Arts at New York University, pursuing her BFA in theater, creative writing and Africana Studies. She was a member of NYU's poetry slam teams in 2011 and 2012, winning first place in the nation. A member of the Dance Cartel, Aziza performs in venues around New York and is finishing a residency at the Ace Hotel. She is a co-founder of the Divine Fabrics Collective. This is her first chapbook.